For Spike the dog and Teddy the bear—our childhood cohorts. —J. L. & J. M.

For my dad. Lover of the earth and mower of the grass upon it. —B. R.

STERLING CHILDREN'S BOOKS
New York

An Imprint of Sterling Publishing
1166 Avenue of the Americas
New York NY 10036

STERLING CHILDREN'S BOOKS and the distinctive Sterling Children's
Books logo are trademarks of Sterling Publishing Co., Inc.

Text, lyrics, and music © 2016 by The Okee Dokee Brothers—Joe Mailander and Justin Lansing
Illustrations © 2016 by Brandon Reese
The artwork for this book was created using Adobe Illustrator and Photoshop.

ISBN 978-1-4549-1803-5

Distributed in Canada by Sterling Publishing
c/o Canadian Manda Group, 664 Annette Street
Toronto, Ontario, Canada M6S 2C8
Distributed in the United Kingdom by GMC Distribution Services
Castle Place, 166 High Street, Lewes, East Sussex, England BN7 1XU
Distributed in Australia by Capricorn Link (Australia) Pty. Ltd.
P.O. Box 704, Windsor, NSW 2756, Australia

For information about custom editions, special sales, and premium and corporate purchases,
please contact Sterling Special Sales at 800-805-5489 or specialsales@sterlingpublishing.com.

Art direction and design by Merideth Harte

Manufactured in China

Lot #:
2 4 6 8 10 9 7 5 3 1
02/16
www.sterlingpublishing.com

THE OKEE DOKEE BROTHERS

CAN YOU CANOE?

AND OTHER ADVENTURE SONGS

ILLUSTRATIONS BY

BRANDON REESE

STERLING CHILDREN'S BOOKS
New York

Note from the Authors

Hello, Reader!

So far, so good—you got the book open. Now, do you want to know a little secret about this thing? The ideas on these pages, they didn't come from our heads. Nope. We had to go searching for them. Where, you ask? Well, that was the fun part. They were hiding among the trees along the Appalachian Trail, floating in the waters of the Mississippi River, and blowing around the peaks on the Continental Divide. We decided to gather them up, write them down, and pass them on, so you can visit those places in your imagination or maybe even in real life.

And speaking of real life, we might look like cartoons here in this book, but guess what? We're real-life people! And we take real-life adventures where we explore real-life places! We actually went on three different month-long camping adventures in order to find inspiration for these songs and to learn a thing or two about ourselves and the great outdoors.

While we hiked through the Appalachian Mountains, we discovered that carrying a tune is a lot more enjoyable than carrying a 40-pound backpack. Canoeing down Old Muddy, we learned to go with the flow and enjoy the current moment. And during our horsepacking trip out West, we realized that horses are a lot like people: You can't control them, but you can learn how to work together to get someplace beautiful.

As you may have noticed, this book doesn't run on a battery, it can't be plugged in, and you can't connect it to the Internet. So, we hope you'll take this book outside. Camp with it. Throw it in the dirt. Read it in a tree. Use it as an umbrella. Forget it at your friend's house. Heck, see if it can fly. Just take it on an adventure, will ya? And while you're at it, see if you can find some new ideas or songs to add to your own story. We know they're out there—trust us, you just have to step outside.

Joe + Justin

—Joe Mailander and Justin Lansing
THE OKEE DOKEE BROTHERS

THROUGH THE WOODS

I'm wondering if you'd go wandering with me
Through the wilderness and woods
To where the winds are blowin' free,
Through the darkness of the night
Headin' toward the morning light
I WONDER IF YOU'D WANDER WITH ME.

I'll spread the word
And you beat the drum.
We'll round up the troops
And get the gang to come.
We'll leave the streets
And these neighborhoods—
Head over the river
And through the woods.

You're wondering if I go wandering with you
What kind of trouble we'll get ourselves into.
Would it be wrong to tag along
With a band of vagabonds?
YOU WONDER IF I'D WANDER WITH YOU.

CHORUS

I'm wondering if you'd come wandering my way,
If you ever get lost
Or if the trail leads you astray.
The music of the pack
Can always bring ya back.
I WONDER—CAN WE WANDER AWAY?

CHORUS

Jamboree

There's a country store
In a country town.
Every Friday night
The people dance around.
It don't look like much
And it ain't no chore,
But while they're dancin'
They polish that floor.

They play this song
Right on key.
They play this song—
It's called "Jamboree."

There's a little old lady
Plays a big old bass.
And that banjo maybe
Should have stayed in the case.
And the guitar there
Has a broken string.
And the fiddle's flyin'
And everyone sings.

They play this song
Almost on key.
They play this song—
It's called "Jamboree."

Fleas in your pants,
Coals on the floor.
S'pose you can dance
If you can count to four.
So grab you a partner
And hold on tight
'Cause we ain't stoppin'
Until we see the light.

We'll play this song
Way off key.
We'll play this song—
It's called "Jamboree."

BLACK BEAR MAMA

We were out having our Jamboree
In a little clearing in the dogwood trees,
Eating biscuits and black-eyed peas—
Pipin' hot and steamin'.

Black Bear Mama came out of her den.
She left the little ones 8, 9, 10.
Sayin', "Don't you worry, I'll come back again.
And we'll have supper this evenin'."

She eats honey, from a honeybee.
She eats it on biscuits, but she don't eat me.

Black Bear Mama going 'round the woods
Lookin' for something that'll taste so good.
Black Bear Mama playin' Robin Hood
To feed her poor little children.

When she found us she looked pretty mean
And we didn't feel like makin' a scene,
So we made a donation of pork and beans
Before we got our fillin'.

You better run from the **foldy** rolly tilly tolly
Seeka dubba yoosa 'cause a bear's gonna find you.

She eats honey, from a honeybee.
She eats it on biscuits, but she don't eat me.

Black Bear Mama went back to her den
To feed the little ones 8, 9, 10.
They ate it all up in a gulp, and then
In a minute they were snoring.

But Black Bear Mama had a hungry pack—
Our campfire cookin' was just a snack.
They woke up Mama, said, "You better go back
For hotcakes in the morning."

They ate honey, from a honeybee.
They ate it on biscuits, but they didn't eat me.

Yeah, they ate honey, they ate the black-eyed pea,
They ate it with biscuits, but they didn't eat me.

I came across a valley
With a wide mountain view,
And sang out your name
With yodel-odle-ay-hee-hoo.

YODEL-AY-HEE-HOO (yodel-ay-hee-hoo)
YODEL-AY-HEE-HEE (yodel-ay-hee-hee)
YODEL-AY-HEE-HOO (yodel-ay-hee-hoo)
I'm in love with you!

I fell asleep that evening
Singin' up to the night.
And that valley was so wide
I heard the echo in the morning light.

CHORUS

Then came along a rich man—
Richer than a king.
He tried to buy my song,
But money can't make me sing.

Ya know love is like an echo—
If it's pure and it's true,
Then sing it out to the world
And it'll come back to you.

YODEL-AY-HEE-HOO (yodel-ay-hee-hoo)
YODEL-AY-HEE-HEE (yodel-ay-hee-hee)
YODEL-AY-HEE-HOO (yodel-ay-hee-hoo)
I'm still in love with you-
I'm still in love with you!
I'm still in love with you!

The Bullfrog Opera

We're sleeping out in the forest again,
Far from the cities and the streets.
But if we close our eyes and we improvise,
We can make it to *New York* in our dreams.
The moon becomes a streetlamp in *Central Park*,
And the river is a train *Brooklyn*-bound.
The stars turn into pearls on high-heeled girls,
Getting ready for a night on the town.

Let's take 'em to The Bullfrog Opera
And the raccoon's masquerade ball.
We've got *Broadway* tickets to see a chorus line of crickets,
And the loons are playing *Carnegie Hall*.

Our tent starts looking like the *Plaza Hotel*—
Tonight we'll sleep like we're rich.
The trees grow to equate the size of the *Empire State*,
And the trail becomes the *Triborough Bridge*.
We're sitting front row at nature's symphony show
With the winds, the reeds, and the strings.
We wait for the piano to cue the soprano
'Cause it's not over till the fat lady sings.

She's singing in The Bullfrog Opera
And the raccoon's masquerade ball.
We've got *Broadway* tickets to see a chorus line of crickets,
And the loons are playing *Carnegie Hall*.

CAMPIN' TENT

I got myself in trouble
When I bought myself a **home**.
'Cause I thought myself a millionaire,
But then I couldn't pay off the loan.
So I moved down to the river,
Where fishin' hooks pay the rent.
And now I'm livin' off of rice and beans,
And sleepin' in my campin' tent—
My campin' tent . . .

It's my transportable, affordable **apartment**,
Where I open the roof zipper and can
Watch the Big Dipper risin' as a
Breeze blows through the window vent.
It's time well spent—livin' in my campin' tent.

Well, I always thought a **mansion**
Would be a nice abode.
But in the fine print that I read it said that
You couldn't take it on the road.
So now whenever I want to leave,
I go wherever I can live in peace.
'Cause whoever wants to live in a campin' tent
Never has to sign a lease.

It might have a rather low ceiling,
But it keeps me humble 'cause I'm always kneeling.
And if it rains, I can trust my roof
'Cause this **wigwam** is waterproof.

I love my campin' tent . . .

CHORUS

I used to have toys and trinkets,
And knickknacks layin' around.
And while those things are nice to have,
They end up weighin' you down.
So I left all my belongings,
'Cause they made me discontent.
And the only thing I brought with me
Was this little old **campin' tent** . . .

CHORUS

My campin' tent . . .
It's my transportable, affordable apartment.
It's foldable, holdable, easily moldable,
Totable, boatable, probably even floatable,
Dependable, mendable—the poles are pretty bendable—
Enjoyable, deployable, but doesn't have a toilet bowl—
Big ol' campin' tent.

Can You Canoe?

We don't need a motor;
We don't need a sail.
And we don't need no fins or gills,
And we don't need a tail.
Let's just keep it simple–
We'll each get an oar,
Paddle out to No Man's Lake,
And float till we can't no more.

Can you canoe on a little boat built for two?
Can you canoe? I'll be your captain and your crew.
Can you canoe if there's nothin' better to do?
I wanna float down a river with you.

We don't need no outlets;
We don't need no wires.
Prime-time entertainment
Will be lightnin' bugs and fires.
Let's just keep it simple–
Unplugged and outside.
Sound waves on the water
Don't need to be amplified.

CHORUS

I'll take the bow, brother;
You can take the stern.
I'll move us forward,
And you choose when to turn.
Let's just keep it simple–
We all need a friend
In this current moment,
Instead of lookin' around the bend.

CHORUS

I wanna float down a river with you.
I wanna float down a river with you.

Mr. & Mrs. Sippy

Mr. and Mrs. Sippy
Got married in the fall.
They left the church that very same day
For their honeymoon in St. Paul,
Singin' *M-I-double-S-I-double-S-I-P-P-I*
M-I-double-S-I-double-S-I-P-P-I.

Mr. and Mrs. Sippy—
They rambled and they roamed.
But when they got down to St. Louie,
They made themselves a home,
Singin' *M-I-double-S-I-double-S-I-P-P-I*
M-I-double-S-I-double-S-I-P-P-I.

Mr. and Mrs. Sippy
Were traveling southbound.
They had some kids and raised 'em
In good old Memphis Town.

Mr. and Mrs. Sippy
Had no place left to go.
So they drifted down past New Orleans
To the Gulf of Mexico,
Singin' *M-I-double-S-I-double-S-I-P-P-I*
M-I-double-S-I-double-S-I-P-P-I.

You can't find me—**1** Mississippi, **2** Mississippi, **3**,
4 Mississippi, **5** Mississippi, *olly olly oxen free*!

Sing it backwards!
I-P-P-I-double-S-I-double-S-I-M
I-P-P-I-double-S-I-double-S-I-M.

Sing it forward!
M-I-double-S-I-double-S-I-P-P-I
M-I-double-S-I-double-S-I-P-P-I.

THE GREAT DIVIDE

There's a great divide that makes the rivers and the rains
Flow to the western ocean or run through the eastern plains.
So you go **east**, and I go **west**—
You go where the sun rises, and I go where it sets.

When I'm down in the valley
On my side of the line,
It's hard to know that your hill
Is the same as mine.
And that mountaintop between us
Is the only place to see the other side.
So let's meet up in the middle,
Along the great divide.

The road is ROCKY; the trail is STEEP.
The cliffs get higher where the river runs deep.
And it's not easy to look at what divides us,
But if we do, we might find it's the same thing that unites us.

CHORUS

Up above the tree line **two** paths become **one**.
And as we ride together, **two** sides become **none**.
Finding common ground is a tricky thing to do,
But on the top of a mountain we can share a point of view.

CHORUS

The Legend of Tall Talkin' Sam

I was born to a pioneer woman
And a Rocky Mountain mountain man.
They named me Samantha Rosie-Anna,
But I told 'em I go by Sam.
Had spurs on my boots, a whip in my hand,
Didn't wail or scream or cry.
I come out a ridin' a panther,
Ropin' a twister outta the sky.

My pillow is the Big Horn Mountains,
I use a blanket of snow if I gotta.
I lay my hat down in Montana
And my boots in Colorada.
When I start to get tired,
Which happens 'bout once a week,
I blow out the moonlight,
And sing the wolves to sleep.

Sure I might be . . .
Tall talkin', loud squawkin'—
Gotta tell it tall to tell it right.
Showboatin', misquotin'—
My tall tales are larger than life.

I outran old Davy Crockett
From Oregon to Delaware,
'Cause I'm half horse, half mountain lion,
Half grizzly bear.
I won an arm wrestlin' match
Against the legendary Pecos Bill.
He said, "That gal's got more grit
Than anyone ever will!"

CHORUS

But there's one thing that's for certain,
And I'm sure you'll think it's so:
There's too much in this old world
Even a girl like me don't know.
Like how some little stream
Carved out one big ol' canyon,
Or how a fire's angry flame
Can be your best companion.
Why lookin' up at the stars
Will always make you feel small.
Why just telling the truth
Ain't tellin' the whole story at all.

That's why we're always . . .
Tall talkin', loud squawkin'—
Gotta tell it tall to tell it right.
So, if you got a tale to tell,
Talk it tall and tell it well,
'Cause this world is larger than life.
Yeah, this world is larger than life.

JACKALOPE

There's a mysterious animal I'm lookin' for—
They call it the jackalope.
It's got the body of a jackrabbit
And the antlers of an antelope.

Some say they're fast, and some say they're slow.
I've heard they're big; I've heard they're small.
Seems like no one can ever agree—
IT'S ALMOST LIKE THEY DON'T EXIST AT ALL.

They're only seen between midnight and two
On leap years, beneath a blue moon.
When it's hot on the tundra and snowing in the desert
On the thirty-first of June.

Well, I've seen 'em in books and in taxidermy shops;
I've seen 'em hangin' on the wall.
But I ain't never seen one in the livin' light of day—
IT'S ALMOST LIKE THEY DON'T EXIST AT ALL.

So when you're searchin' for the truth,
And you're at the end of your rope,
You might find you don't need no proof
To believe in the thing that gives you hope—
And for me, that's the jackalope.

SADDLE UP

Saddle up, settle in—
Every story must begin,
And this one is tall but it's true.
It starts as a quest
To tell the tales of the West,
And how it ends, well, nobody knows but you.

Tell us a good one tonight
While the fire's burnin' bright,
'Bout mountains and rivers of gold.
Sing us a good one tonight
'Neath the moon's silver light,
Full of tall tales and legends of old.

Hunker down, gather round—
Roll the blankets out on the ground
As our shadows grow taller than trees.
There ain't nothin' for miles,
So the stories run wild,
And the songs can roam anywhere they please.

CHORUS

Move 'em out, move 'em in—
Every story has to end.
But some stay in your heart—
They go round and round;
They get lost and then found,
'Cause the end is just another place to start.

The Okee Dokee Brothers' Field Journal:
A Song-by-Song Guide

THROUGH THE WOODS

Seems like every journey begins with a question . . . or at least some wondering. With this song, we started by wondering what it would be like to leave our neighborhood, grab a friend, and wander along the Appalachian Trail with our guitar and banjo. Well, there was really only one way to find out, and that was to get out there and start hiking, right through the woods.

JAMBOREE

While we were out there wandering, we came across the infamous Friday Nite Jamboree. It's held in an old country store where people in town get together and do a special kind of dancing called clogging (some call it flat-footin'). There were all different kinds of people there and a great old-time band playing guitars, banjos, fiddles, and a big ol' bass. Young and old, everyone danced—including us! Luckily, Joe took a few lessons on how to clog before we left for the trip. Unluckily, Justin did not . . . but he was equally entertaining out there on the dance floor!

BLACK BEAR MAMA

Before setting out on this journey, we read all sorts of books about the wildlife around the Appalachian Trail. They always seemed to mention one thing for certain: black bears. So naturally, we kept our eyes peeled around every turn just in case. One night, Joe heard what he thought was a black bear rustling and growling around the campsite, but it just turned out to be Justin snoring—loudly!

ECHO

We saw some of the best mountain-top views on the trail, and every time we reached a look-out, we made sure to do some yodeling. You know, just to see if we could hear our echoes bounce back from the other side of those valleys. It really makes you think about how words and actions can come back to us just like echoes do. So we figured we might as well sing out something positive.

THE BULLFROG OPERA

We wrote part of this song while living in New York City, and the other part while canoeing down the Mississlppi River. You can probably tell that we were jumping from place to place in our imaginations, and bridging the best of both worlds. We found that even when you're in a big city surrounded by buildings and concrete, there are still lots of places to find nature. Sometimes, you just have to look a little closer.

CAMPIN' TENT

Herc's an ode to the most wonderful abode. When you're out exploring all day, the best feeling in the world is to reach camp, eat some grub, set up your campin' tent, and let the snooze-fest begin. Then, after a good night's sleep, you really notice how waking up in a tent is somehow different than waking up in a bed. Maybe it's the fresh air, maybe it's the heat of the sun on the tent, or maybe it's the spider that slept beside you all night. That'll sure wake you up quick!

CAN YOU CANOE?

Now, that's a good question. Can any of you out there canoe? Have you ever been on a canoe or seen a canoe? Good. Then you know what we're talking about. They're boats. But they don't have motors and they don't have sails. They do have . . . what? That's right. Paddles. So get your paddles out, and imagine you're floating down a river with one of your best friends as you listen to this song.

MR. & MRS. SIPPY

On our Mississippi adventure, we met a couple who lived on the river. They loved that river so much that it inspired us to write a love song about them. See, their love started small, like the beginning of the Mississippi, but around each little bend it grew into a life full of friends and family.

THE GREAT DIVIDE

The Great Divide is just another way of saying the Continental Divide. In case you were wondering, the Continental Divide is an imaginary line made up of some of the highest peaks in the Rocky Mountains, starting way up in Alaska and ending in the Andes of South America. The rivers on the east side flow to the Atlantic Ocean, and the rivers on the west side flow to the Pacific Ocean. We had been riding horses all day, thinking about the common ground in our friendship. We stopped to rest right on top of the Great Divide in Colorado, and that's where we wrote some of the words to this song.

THE LEGEND OF TALL TALKIN' SAM

We met up with our friend, Pecos Bill, while we were in Wyoming. Caught him right in the middle of ropin' a tornado headed for Texas! We asked him about the roughest, toughest, most hootin' and hollerin', wildest and craziest person he knew. He told us the tale of Samantha Rosie-Anna, and according to him, Tall Talkin' Sam was larger than life itself!

JACKALOPE

We've been on the lookout for a real-life North American jackalope. We've searched high and low. They're tricky to see 'cause they're quicker than lightnin'. They're impossible to hear 'cause their feet are as soft as fresh moss. And they're hard to catch 'cause they can escape any trap. Some people don't believe they exist, but if you ask us, those people are probably just jackalopes in disguise.

SADDLE UP

Ahhh, nothin' beats a good campfire. It's the perfect place to unwind and tell a few tales. Whether they're from last week, last year, or hundreds of years ago, a good story can take you anywhere. They all seem to weave together, too, and where one story ends, another one begins.

About the Creators

THE OKEE DOKEE BROTHERS

JOE MAILANDER and **JUSTIN LANSING** have known each other since they were three years old. As childhood friends growing up in Denver, Colorado, they were always exploring the outdoors. Whether it was rafting down their neighborhood creek or discovering hiking trails through the Rocky Mountains, Joe and Justin were born adventurers. They started playing music together in high school, and now, as the GRAMMY® Award–winning Okee Dokee Brothers, they have put their passion for the outdoors at the heart of their Americana folk music.

Joe and Justin make family music and take real-life adventures with a goal to inspire families to get outside and get creative. They believe this can motivate families to gain a greater respect for the natural world, for their communities, and for themselves. Learn more about them at okeedokee.org.

THE ILLUSTRATOR

BRANDON REESE created the distinctive cover artwork for The Okee Dokee Brothers' albums, and is also the illustrator for a number of clients including Nickelodeon, Nick Jr., eeBoo, BOOM! Studios, and more. Brandon lives in North Carolina with his wife and young son. Learn more about him online at brandonreese.com.

Credits

THROUGH THE WOODS
Joe Mailander guitar, vocals
Justin Lansing banjo, vocals
Jed Anderson percussion, vocals
Dean Jones vocals
Mark Murphy upright bass
David Holt slide guitar, harmonica
Rosie Newton fiddle

JAMBOREE
Justin Lansing vocals
Joe Mailander guitar, vocals
Jed Anderson percussion, vocals
Dean Jones vocals
Mark Murphy upright bass, vocals
Amy Fenton-Shine clogging
David Holt banjo
Hubby Jenkins vocals
Rosie Newton fiddle, vocals

BLACK BEAR MAMA
Justin Lansing banjo, vocals
Joe Mailander vocals
Jed Anderson percussion
Dean Jones vocals, tuba
Mark Murphy upright bass
David Holt fingerstyle guitar, jaw harp

ECHO
Joe Mailander guitar, vocals
Justin Lansing banjo, vocals
Jed Anderson percussion, vocals
Dean Jones percussion, harmonica
Mark Murphy upright bass
Paul McMahon yodels
Hubby Jenkins vocals
Andrea Maddox vocals

THE BULLFROG OPERA
Joe Mailander guitar, vocals
Justin Lansing vocals
Jed Anderson percussion, vocals
Dean Jones trombone
Mark Murphy upright bass
Morgan Taylor vocals
Jeremy Mage piano, organ
David Winograd tuba

CAMPIN' TENT
Joe Mailander guitar, vocals
Justin Lansing banjo, vocals
Jed Anderson percussion
Dean Jones vocals, glockenspiel
Jeremy Mage piano
David Winograd tuba

CAN YOU CANOE?
Justin Lansing banjo, vocals
Joe Mailander guitar, vocals
Jed Anderson percussion, vocals
Mark Murphy upright bass
Ken McGloin slide guitar

MR. & MRS. SIPPY
Justin Lansing banjo, vocals
Joe Mailander guitar, vocals
Jed Anderson percussion
Dean Jones whistling
Jeremy Mage piano, organ
David Winograd tuba
Wayne Montecalvo fiddle
Ken McGloin slide guitar
Max and Nadia Welden kid vocals

THE GREAT DIVIDE
Joe Mailander guitar, vocals
Justin Lansing banjo, vocals
Jed Anderson percussion
Mark Murphy upright bass
Jeremy Mage piano
Jim Campilongo electric guitar
Rosie Newton fiddle
John Burdick electric guitar

THE LEGEND OF TALL TALKIN' SAM
Justin Lansing banjo, vocals
Joe Mailander guitar, vocals
Jed Anderson percussion
Dean Jones second guitar
Rosie Newton fiddle, vocals
Mark Murphy upright bass

JACKALOPE
Justin Lansing banjo, vocals
Joe Mailander guitar, vocals
Jed Anderson percussion
Dean Jones jaw harp
Mark Murphy upright bass
Jim Campilongo electric guitar
Jeremy Mage organ
Rosie Newton vocals
Rachel Loshak vocals
Guy "Fooch" Fischetti pedal steel

SADDLE UP
Joe Mailander guitar, vocals
Justin Lansing banjo, vocals
Jed Anderson percussion
Mark Murphy upright bass
Rosie Newton fiddle
John Sebastian harmonica
Cindy Cashdollar dobro
Guy "Fooch" Fischetti pedal steel

All songs written by Justin Lansing and Joe Mailander

All songs produced, mixed, and engineered by Dean Jones

All songs mastered by Alan Douches and West West Side Music

Special thanks to Jennifer Mattson, Dean Jones, Casey Peterson, Jed Anderson, Hanna Otero-Bird, Meredith Mundy, Zaneta Jung, Kim Broderick, Merideth Harte, Sari Lampert, Lauren Tambini, and the rest of the gang at Sterling Children's Books.

More music and live concert info:
okeedokee.org
Music videos and adventure films:
youtube.com/okeedokeebros
Facebook: facebook.com/okeedokeebros
Instagram: instagram.com/okeedokeebros
Twitter: twitter.com/okeedokeebros

Management:
Dandelion Artists
Sarah McCarthy
Los Angeles, CA
sarah@dandelionartists.com

CONTINENTAL
DIVIDE

WASHINGTON

OREGON

MONTANA

NORTH
DAKOTA

Saddle UP

IDAHO

SOUTH
DAKOTA

WYOMING

• The Legend of
Tall Talkin' Sam

NEBRASKA

NEVADA

CALIFORNIA

UTAH

COLORADO

• The Great
Divide

KA

PACIFIC OCEAN

ARIZONA

Jackalope

NEW MEXICO

TEX

MEXICO

N
W   E
S